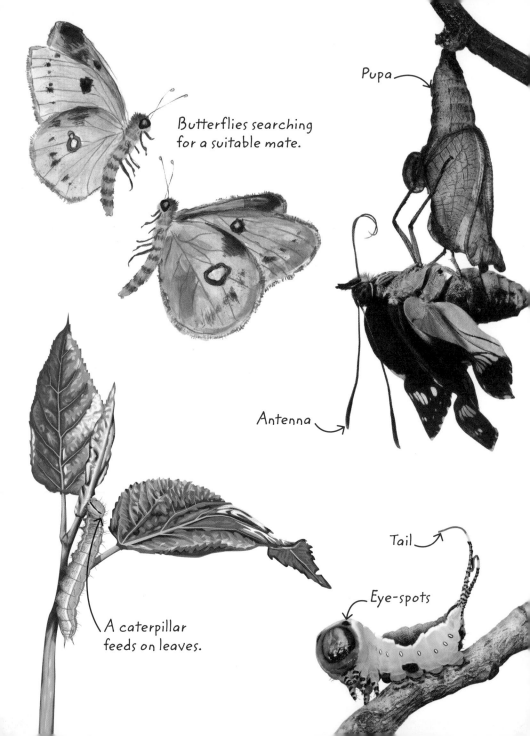

Butterflies searching for a suitable mate.

Pupa

Antenna

A caterpillar feeds on leaves.

Tail

Eye-spots

Butterflies and Moths

Written by John Feltwell

Consultant: Richard Lamb

DK

Senior editors Sam Priddy, Jolyon Goddard
US Editor Jill Hamilton
Editor Radhika Haswani
Senior art editor Fiona Macdonald
Project art editor Rashika Kachroo
Art editor Kanika Kalra
Illustrators Abby Cook, Dan Crisp, Molly Lattin
Jacket coordinator Francesca Young
Jacket designer Rhea Gaughan
DTP designer Sachin Gupta

Senior DTP designer Jagtar Singh
Senior picture researcher Surya Sankash Sarangi
Producer, pre-production Dragana Puvacic
Producer Isabell Schart
Managing editors Laura Gilbert, Monica Saigal
Managing art editor Diane Peyton Jones
Deputy managing art editor Ivy Sengupta
Art director Martin Wilson
Publishing director Sarah Larter

Original edition
Senior editor Susan McKeever
Editor Jodi Block
Assistant editor Djinn von Noorden
Editorial consultant David Carter
Art editor Vicky Wharton
Illustrators Brian Hargreaves, Nick Hewetson,
Tommy Swahn
Production Catherine Semark
Photography by Frank Greenway

First American Edition, 1993
This edition published in the United States in 2018 by DK Publishing
345 Hudson Street, New York, New York 10014

Copyright © 1993, 2018 Dorling Kindersley Limited
DK, a Division of Penguin Random House LLC
18 19 20 21 22 10 9 8 7 6 5 4 3 2 1
001–309698–Mar/2018

A catalog record for this book
is available from the Library of Congress.
ISBN: 978-1-4654-7340-0

DK books are available at special discounts when purchased in bulk
for sales promotions, premiums, fund-raising, or educational use.
For details, contact: DK Publishing Special Markets, 345 Hudson Street, New York, New York 10014
SpecialSales@dk.com

Printed and bound in China

The publisher would like to thank the following for their kind permission to reproduce their photographs:
(Key: a-above; b-below/bottom; c-center; f-far; l-left; r-right; t-top)

4 Dorling Kindersley: Thomas Marent (br). **5 123RF.com:** Juan Aunion. **8 iStockphoto.com:** Vandervelden. **9 123RF.com:** Geza Farkas (cla). **Dreamstime.com:** Yael Weiss (br/Magnifying glass).
10 Dorling Kindersley: Jerry Young. **11 Dreamstime.com:** Stig Karlsson (tr); Qpicimages (t). **iStockphoto.com:** Ian_Redding (cl); Vitakot (br). **12 Getty Images:** Andia / Universal Images Group Editorial (tr).
13 Dreamstime.com: Holger Leyrer / Leyrer (br). **Getty Images:** Stephen Dalton / Minden Pictures (tl). **14 Alamy Stock Photo:** Marco Uliana (crb). **16 iStockphoto.com:** Baku_Retsu (bc). **17 Alamy Stock
Photo:** Rene Krekels / NIS / Minden Pictures (br). **Dreamstime.com:** Ams22 (cla); Brett Critchley / BCritchley (tt). **18 Getty Images:** John Forsdyke / Oxford Scientific (crb). **19 123RF.com:** Snike (t/Sky).
Alamy Stock Photo: Animals / GFC Collection (cl). **iStockphoto.com:** RoseABC (tl). **Science Photo Library:** Bjorn Rorslett (bc); Bjorn Rorslett (br). **20 Getty Images:** Andre Simon / Biosphoto (br).
23 Alamy Stock Photo: Les Gibbon (cl). **iStockphoto.com:** Wichatsurin (br). **24 Dreamstime.com:** Jack Dean (cr). **iStockphoto.com:** HHelene (bl). **25 iStockphoto.com:** TheDman (t). **27 Alamy Stock Photo:**
Blickwinkel (tr); Frank Hecker (cb); David Chapman (bc). **Dorling Kindersley:** Natural History Museum, London (cl). **29 Alamy Stock Photo:** John Glover (bl). **30–31 Dorling Kindersley. 30 Dreamstime.
com:** Susan Elisabeth Bellis (cra). **31 Dorling Kindersley. 32 123RF.com:** Tyler Fox (crb). **Alamy Stock Photo:** Lisa Moore (tl). **33 Alamy Stock Photo:** Frank Hecker (tt). **Dreamstime.com:** David Ford (cr).
iStockphoto.com: Miyuki-3 (cr/Larva of pieris rapae). **34 Alamy Stock Photo:** Nigel Cattlin (tr). **35 Alamy Stock Photo:** Buschkind (crb). **36 Dreamstime.com:** Ian Redding (clb). **37 123RF.com:** Likelike (tr).
Dorling Kindersley. 39 Alamy Stock Photo: Gillian Pullinger (br). **41 123RF.com:** Bunyarit Suwansantawee (cla). **Dreamstime.com:** Sofiaworld (bl); Marinko Tarlac / Mangia (tr). **PunchStock:** Design Pics
(bc). **42 123RF.com:** Helgidinson (cl). **43 123RF.com:** Leekris (ca). **Dreamstime.com:** Gerald Deboer (crb). **44 123RF.com:** Marc Parsons (b). **45 Alamy Stock Photo:** Les Gibbon (cr). **Dreamstime.com:** Yael
Weiss (cl/Magnifying glass). **Getty Images:** Stephen Dalton / Minden Pictures (t). **iStockphoto.com:** Vuk8691 (cl). **47 Dorling Kindersley:** Natural History Museum, London (cl). **Dreamstime.com:** Cathy
Keifer (br). **Getty Images:** W. Perry Conway / Corbis (tr). **49 Alamy Stock Photo:** Andrew Newman Nature Pictures (cl); Richard Becker (tr). **50 Dorling Kindersley:** Natural History Museum, London (clb).
Getty Images: Ger Bosma / Moment (bc). **51 123RF.com:** Christian Wei (cla). **Alamy Stock Photo:** Robert Hurn (bl). **Dorling Kindersley. 52 123RF.com:** Roberta Canu (br). **Dreamstime.com:** Jerryway (tr).
53 123RF.com: Jakub Cejpek (bl); Johnaapw (cr). **Dorling Kindersley:** Natural History Museum, London (tr). **Dreamstime.com:** Ivan Kmit / Ivankmit (t); Tiberiu Sahlean (bc). **54 Dorling Kindersley:** Natural
History Museum, London (cl). **55 123RF.com:** Anusorn Phuengprasert na chol (cra); Abi Warner (br); Juan Aunion (tl). **Getty Images:** Piotr Naskrecki / Minden Pictures (clb). **56 Alamy Stock Photo:** Rick &
Nora Bowers (tr). **Dreamstime.com:** Vladimir Blinov / Vblinov (tr/Background). **Getty Images:** Jasius / Moment (bl). **57 Dreamstime.com:** Geza Farkas (cr). **58 naturepl.com:** Jussi Murtosaari (b).
59 123RF.com: Missisya (cl/Rock). **Alamy Stock Photo:** Rick & Nora Bower (tr); David Hosking (cl)

Cover images: **Front: Dorling Kindersley:** Natural History Museum, London tl, bc; **Dreamstime.com:** Yael Weiss crb; **Science Photo Library:** cra; **Back: Dorling Kindersley:** Natural History Museum,
London cla, ca, cb, cr; **Spine: Dorling Kindersley:** Natural History Museum, London cb, cb/ (Arctia caja)

All other images © Dorling Kindersley
For further information see: www.dkimages.com

A WORLD OF IDEAS:
SEE ALL THERE IS TO KNOW
www.dk.com

Contents

Butterflies and moths

You can spot butterflies and moths fluttering around parks, gardens, and just about anywhere that has wildflowers. Colorful flowers attract lots of butterflies, and you can watch them as they feed on nectar. Look for moths flying around streetlights at night.

Beautiful butterfly

See how many different colors you can find on the wings of a butterfly. Look at the undersides too—the colors are often completely different! You can recognize this painted lady butterfly by the black and white spots on its orange wings.

Look for painted ladies feeding on thistle flowers.

Butterflies, like all insects, breathe through small holes on their bodies.

TAKE NOTE

When looking at butterflies and moths, it is a good idea to make sketches. Draw an outline first, then color in the different patterns. Write down where and when you made the drawing, and anything else that may help you identify the butterfly or moth.

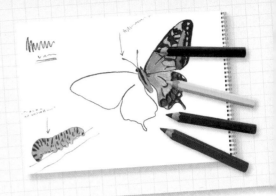

Nighttime flier

Moths are mostly nighttime fliers, but you can also spot them resting on walls, fences, and tree trunks during the day. Most moths are dull colored, but this Jersey tiger moth is unusually bright. Its front wings are striped just like a tiger.

The orange and black colors on this moth's hind wings make it easy to spot.

A closer look

A magnifying glass lets you look at butterflies, moths, and their young (caterpillars) in great detail—up to 10 times bigger than they really are. If you want to pick up a caterpillar from its leaf for a closer look, be sure to use a paintbrush so you do not harm it with your fingers.

 Be careful when using a magnifying glass in sunlight. It can cause fire.

Which is which?

They do not crawl like ants and beetles, but butterflies and moths are insects just the same. They belong to the insect group Lepidoptera, which means scaly wings. Most butterflies are colorful, while moths are normally dull. Moths mostly have thick, hairy bodies, and feathery antennae (feelers), whereas butterfly antennae are long and thin.

Body parts

Like all insects, butterflies and moths have three pairs of legs and three body parts—a head, a thorax, and an abdomen. They also have two large pairs of wings, antennae, and eyes.

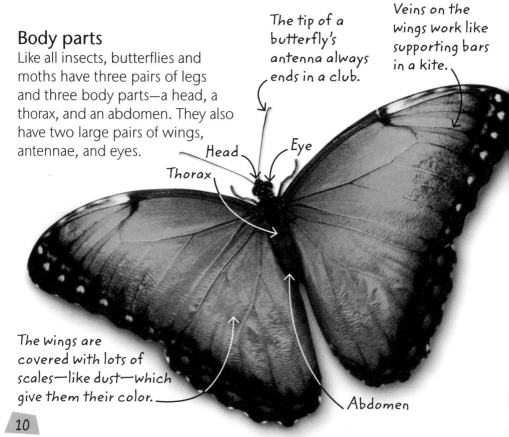

The tip of a butterfly's antenna always ends in a club.

Veins on the wings work like supporting bars in a kite.

Head

Eye

Thorax

The wings are covered with lots of scales—like dust—which give them their color.

Abdomen

Asleep on a leaf

Most moths are small with short wings and a stubby body. When they rest, moths often slide their wings over each other into a triangular shape, so the front pair of wings covers the hind wings.

Front wing

Hind wing

Can you spot the Y-shaped marks on this silver Y moth's wings?

Resting up

A resting butterfly, such as this comma butterfly, claps its big wings together, straight up over its body. Look out for butterflies resting in this position on warm sunny days.

Shape and color help butterflies blend in with their natural surroundings.

Keeping warm

Butterflies and moths have to warm themselves up before they can fly. Daytime fliers bask in the sun. Those that fly at night vibrate their wings to warm up their flight muscles.

Wondrous wings

Butterflies and moths have one thing that no other insects have—scales on their wings. Thousands of tiny scales are delicately arranged on the wings to give them color. Wings carry color-coded messages that help deter enemies and attract mates. Wings of some butterflies flash bright colors in the face of danger to startle predators.

Wings of lace
Some butterflies' wings are plain and brown on top. But if you catch a glimpse of the underside, you may see a beautiful lace pattern.

Flashing color
Left undisturbed, the speckled wings of this red underwing moth blend in perfectly with the background. However, when it is threatened, the moth moves its forewings forward to reveal a bright red warning color.

Look for these moths resting on willow and poplar trees.

When the moth flashes this fiery red band, it confuses predators long enough for the moth to escape.

Scale shower

The moment a butterfly or moth flaps its wings, the scales start to fall off, like a shower of dust. As the insect gets older, it begins to lose its lovely colors and patterns that protect it.

Four eyes

Many butterflies and moths send signals with their wings. The four big, round marks on the peacock butterfly's wings are false eyes that scare birds and lizards away. The bright patterns and false eyes are made up of thousands of scales on the wing.

If you look at the wing close up, it is easy to see the rows of overlapping scales.

The false eye is made up of circles of different colored scales.

The colored scales fade in sunlight, so by the end of the summer this butterfly may not look as bright.

Make a butterfly

Butterfly and moth wings look very thin and fragile, but they are really quite strong. A network of veins supports the wings just like the plastic rods in a kite. You can make your own butterfly or moth kite and decorate the wings with colorful patterns. You'll need paper, scissors, glue, markers, paper straws, and string.

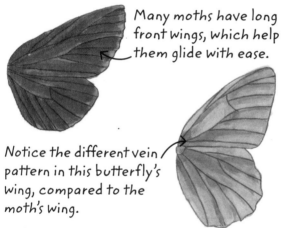

Many moths have long front wings, which help them glide with ease.

Notice the different vein pattern in this butterfly's wing, compared to the moth's wing.

Vein patterns
Butterflies and moths have a special pattern of veins in their wings. This pattern helps scientists identify them. The veins stiffen the wing and keep it in the right position for flying.

Chinese kites
Many Chinese butterflies have big, colorful wings. Thousands of years ago, their beauty and grace inspired expert kite-makers in China.

Paris peacock butterfly

HOW TO BUILD THE KITE

Make the wings about 6 in (15 cm) tall with a 6 in (15 cm) wingspan. The body should be 3 in (8 cm) tall.

Wingspan

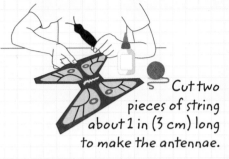

Cut two pieces of string about 1 in (3 cm) long to make the antennae.

1. On a piece of paper, draw the outline and pattern of a butterfly's wings and body. Use markers to make a bright and colorful wing pattern. If you use tissue paper, the color will appear on both sides.

2. Carefully cut out the wings (keeping them joined in the middle) and the body. Then glue the body to the middle of the wings and glue the antennae to the head.

3. Lay a piece of string, about 20 in (50 cm) long, loosely across the wings. Then place two straws over the string and tape them down at the tips so that they form an X. Tie the string firmly around the straws and make a knot.

Now you're ready to fly the kite. Just hold onto the string and run—the butterfly kite will flutter around behind you!

Fluttering and gliding

Depending on the shape of their wings, butterflies and moths make different patterns as they fly. If their wings are long and thin they fly fast and straight, but if they have large wide wings they just flutter about. Some butterflies glide on currents of air—just one flap and they can sail through the sky for a long time.

The female flaps her wings quickly, trying to avoid the male below.

As the male lifts his wings, they push air backward, so that the butterfly moves forward.

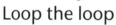

Loop the loop

If you take a walk through a forest glade and see one butterfly looping around another, you may have spotted a pair of silver-washed fritillaries. The male flies below the female, to pass his scents under her antennae. These scents will eventually persuade the female to mate with him.

Light landing

Holding its wings out wide like a parachute, a butterfly gently drops before landing on its legs

Speedy flight

The wings of a jet fighter plane look just like those of a moth. Both have long thin wings that point backward for speedy flight. This death's-head hawk-moth is one of the fastest moths in the world.

When the wings come down, the butterfly moves upward.

The next wing beat will pull the male down below the female once again. He repeats this about four times.

A frightened butterfly or moth can fly over 30 miles (48 km) an hour!

Fight for light

The speckled wood butterfly likes to bask in a sunny spot on the woodland floor. If another butterfly takes this spot, the two fly around and around, bumping into each other many times. The fight does not last long, and the butterfly that was there first usually wins the spiral battle.

Eyes and seeing

Instead of having just two eyes, butterflies and moths have thousands! Each large eye, called a compound eye, is made up of lots of tiny eyes. Each tiny eye sees what is straight ahead of it, which allows the insect to form a complete picture of its surroundings.

Huge eyes

Huge compound eyes allow insects to see all around. Try creeping up on a butterfly—you will be surprised how quickly it spots you and flies away.

Close-up view of a compound eye

Tiny eyes

The tiny eyes are called ommatidia (*om-a-tid-ee-a*). Each eye forms a small picture. The insect's brain then puts all the pictures together.

Each tiny ommatidium has a clear surface that lets in light.

Bright lights, big risk

Look for nighttime moths fluttering around windows and streetlights. Moths are attracted to light, but become a target for bats that swoop around the bulb, snapping up an easy meal.

Pseudopupil

Spotty eyes

When they are alive, butterflies and moths often have a dark pattern of little spots, called pseudopupils (sud-o-pupils), on their eyes. No one knows exactly why they are there. However, when the insect dies, the pseudopupils fade.

Invisible lines

The light from the Sun that comes after purple on the rainbow is called ultraviolet light. We cannot see this light, but butterflies and moths can. Some flowers, such as this lesser celandine, have ultraviolet stripes on their petals that insects use to guide them to the tasty nectar.

Normal light   UV light

Smelling and sipping

They may not have a nose like we do, but butterflies and moths have an amazing sense of smell. They use their antennae to detect scents—sometimes as far as 2 miles (3 km) away. Most butterflies and moths have a long tongue, called a proboscis, that they use for sipping nectar and other liquids. Look for them fluttering around flowers as they feed.

The antennae are divided into segments.

A butterfly keeps its proboscis rolled up like a spring until it is ready to feed.

Smell detectors
Butterflies need huge antennae to detect flowers and to find other butterflies. Each antenna has thousands of tiny holes that absorb smells.

Long straws
A butterfly's tongue is just like a straw. But it has to uncoil it in order to get to the sweet liquids that lie at the bottom of flowers.

ATTRACTING MOTHS

The sweet smell of sugar attracts moths. To see this, coat a tree trunk or fence with a sugary mixture. Use some old molasses or honey mixed with a bit of water to make a thick gooey mess.

⚠️ Ask an adult to accompany you.

1. With a paintbrush, brush this mixture onto a tree trunk at dusk on a summer night.

2. Using a flashlight, check for moths every half hour. Ants and beetles will come to visit, too.

Extra long tongue
The tongue of this Darwin's hawk-moth is incredibly long, even longer than its body. However it fits neatly into this flower, where it sucks up sugary liquids.

Having a drink
Butterflies drink in all sorts of places. You may spot one at the edge of a puddle or in the mud. This butterfly is drinking sap oozing from a log.

Scientist Charles Darwin thought there must be a flower with an extra long tube to hold this moth's proboscis—and he was right!

Looking at legs

Like all insects, butterflies and moths have three pairs of legs, which are attached to the thorax. Each leg is divided into four different sections hinged to each other for easy movement. They use their legs for walking and for landing on leaves and flowers. Once they've landed, they use their feet to taste the leaves.

When at rest, this moth keeps its legs perfectly still and pretends to be a dead leaf.

Spiky spines
This eyed hawk-moth has tiny backward-facing spines on the lower part of its six legs. They dig in if an enemy attacks.

Muscular femur (thigh)

Hinge joint

The tibia (lower leg) has lots of hairs and spines.

Leg shell
Look for three pairs of legs at the front of a caterpillar's body. These become the true legs of a butterfly or moth. The adult's leg muscles are on the inside of a tough shell called an exoskeleton. The leg ends in a claw for gripping twigs.

Happy landing

Moths use all six of their legs when they come in for a landing. But about half the world's butterflies land on only four legs. The other, weaker pair is tucked under the insect's head.

Front legs look like little brushes.

This brown butterfly has six legs, but uses only four for landing.

Keeping clean

Moths have to keep their antennae in very good condition in order to detect smells. This moth is using its leg to clean its antenna. Each antenna has lots of little shelves that collect pollen from flowers. The stiff spines and hairs on the leg work like a comb to remove the pollen.

Taste test

Many butterflies and moths have special cells on the tips of their feet that they use for tasting leaves. They only need to touch down for a few seconds to identify the plant. If the leaf passes the taste test, then they can lay their eggs on it.

23

Getting together

Have you ever noticed a pair of butterflies or moths flying in circles around one another? Flying like this allows them to smell each other. By smelling special body scents called pheromones (*fer-o-mones*), they can identify a mate of the right species. If the smell is right, the couple will mate. Finding the right mate is called courting.

Mud-puddling

Male butterflies gather on riverbanks to drink water that is rich in mineral salts. These salts help butterflies make special smells to attract a mate.

Pheromones are usually present in tiny scent scales on wings.

Some male moths have large, feathery antennae that can smell a female up to 3 miles (5 km) away!

In hot climates, mud-puddling is a common sight.

I'm over here!

Male moths release smells by thrusting out pencil hairs from their bodies. These hairs scatter the pheromones on the breeze, where females will smell them.

Joined together

These butterflies are mating. They will stay like this, out of danger in the bushes, for several hours. Afterwards, the male flies away and the female lays her eggs.

This female's wings have special colors and patterns to attract male butterflies.

The male butterfly has a pair of claspers that encloses the female's rear end.

Dancing in the sky

Keep a lookout for butterflies or moths dancing and fluttering around each other on warm summer days. A courting couple may fly together for over an hour.

25

All about eggs

Butterfly and moth eggs come in many shapes and sizes, but they are all the first stage in an insect's life. The female lays her eggs on or near the right plant that will be food for the caterpillar when it hatches. This plant is known as the foodplant.

The cycle of life

Butterflies and moths pass through four stages during their lives. They begin as eggs and then hatch into caterpillars. When fully grown, the caterpillars form a pupa, which produces an adult. These changes are called metamorphosis.

The moth curls her abdomen around to put each egg in place.

Laying eggs

As this female comet moth lays her eggs, she glues them to the stem so that they do not fall off. Some moths produce special hairs to put on the eggs to protect them from ants.

Egg identity

Some butterflies and moths lay more than 1,000 eggs, all together. But the red admiral butterfly only lays one egg on each nettle leaf. You can identify a red admiral egg by the eight to ten little ridges around the edge.

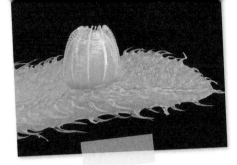

This little group of eggs will hatch into tiny caterpillars and start to nibble on the leaf.

Egg hunt

Search for groups of eggs on leaves, twigs, and buds. They are usually on the underside of leaves and their color may blend in with the leaf—so look carefully.

Falling eggs

A few kinds of butterfly drop their eggs over the grass as they fly along. Wherever the eggs fall they stick. Luckily, the caterpillars that hatch like to eat grass!

The female marbled white butterfly flies low over the grass so that her eggs will hit their grassy target.

Eggs or plant?

This lackey moth disguises her eggs by gluing them around a twig. Other insects and spiders are tricked into thinking that they are just part of the plant.

Caterpillar birth

Being born is a dangerous start to a caterpillar's life. It has only a few minutes to emerge from the egg and hide away from hungry predators. Once it is safely hidden, it begins a life of nonstop eating. If a red admiral caterpillar is lucky, it will live for about a month before it becomes a butterfly.

Eggs with a sting

Look for the red admiral near stinging nettles. It lays single eggs on the top of the nettle leaves.

Ready to go

At first, the pale green egg is full of liquid that looks a bit like soup. A tiny caterpillar is growing inside the liquid. After about 7 days, the egg becomes very dark—it is now ready to hatch.

The caterpillar's body is curled up inside the egg.

Caterpillars can take from a few days to a few years to develop, depending on their species.

Ribbed surface helps the egg keep its shape.

Opening the egg

The tiny caterpillar already has tough jaws. It munches a circle around the top of the egg, and then it rests for a while. You can see the hairy black head poking out of the top.

Out in the open

Curled up tightly for so long, the new caterpillar now pulls itself out of the egg like a jack-in-the-box. It stretches out in the open for the first time.

The old egg case is now transparent. Can you see the supporting ribs on both sides?

Green screen

As soon as it hatches, the caterpillar pulls the sides of the leaf together with silk threads. This shelter hides it from predators. While hiding, the caterpillar eats its first nettle-leaf meal.

The leaf contains minerals that the caterpillar needs to grow and eventually become an adult butterfly.

Camping caterpillar

Look for leaf tents in gardens—you may find a red admiral caterpillar inside! The caterpillar spends its whole life hidden in the tent. During this time, it sheds its skin four times to get bigger.

Clever caterpillars

Birds, lizards, and mammals love the taste of caterpillars. So caterpillars have developed plenty of ways to keep these enemies away. Some disguise themselves as snakes, or show off a pair of big scary eyes. Other caterpillars can blast a nasty-smelling spray into the face of hungry predators.

Small snake?
The caterpillar puffs up the front of its body and shows off its false eyes to trick birds into thinking it is a snake.

Zebra with horns
If you thought only large animals have horns, then look again! The head horns and long spiny hairs on this zebra caterpillar warn predators that an attack might be painful.

Simple eyes at the side of their head allow caterpillars to make out light and dark.

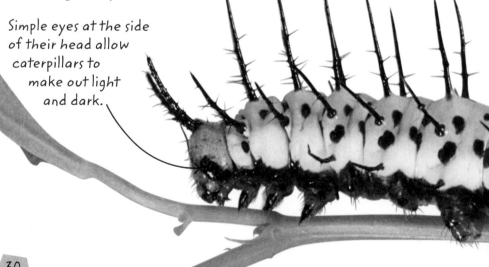

30

Looping along

These caterpillars are called loopers because of the way they move. They hold on with their back legs and move the front end as far away as possible. Then they bring the rear end up to the front so that it forms a loop. Look for loopers on twigs and leaves in the spring.

Do not disturb

When disturbed, these caterpillars flick their bodies into the air. If they all do it together and quickly, it surprises birds and lizards.

Be careful—this caterpillar can spit acid in an enemy's face.

Tail

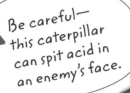

Eye-spots

Fierce face

When danger threatens, the puss moth caterpillar flashes the bright red markings on its face and swings its tail in the air.

Poisonous, spiky horns keep enemies away.

Blending in

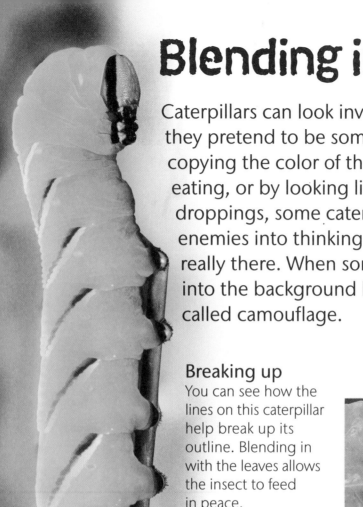

Caterpillars can look invisible when they pretend to be something else. By copying the color of the food they are eating, or by looking like twigs or bird droppings, some caterpillars fool their enemies into thinking that they aren't really there. When something blends into the background like this, it is called camouflage.

Breaking up

You can see how the lines on this caterpillar help break up its outline. Blending in with the leaves allows the insect to feed in peace.

Look for privet hawk-moth caterpillars feeding on leaves in the summer.

Is it or isn't it?

This shiny black swallowtail caterpillar looks exactly like a bird dropping. Now imagine you are a hungry bird—would you risk a bite?

Twiggy disguise

Peppered moth caterpillars look like twigs. They have no legs in the middle of the body and are the same shape and color as the twigs.

Little and large

Poisonous large white caterpillars do not need to hide because enemies know to keep away. Tasty small white caterpillars are camouflaged to stay alive.

At first, small white caterpillars feed unseen on the cabbage.

MIX AND MATCH

Caterpillars come in many different colors and may change color as they get older. Paint a caterpillar outline and fill it in with yellow paint. Then add some blue paint. What color is your caterpillar now?

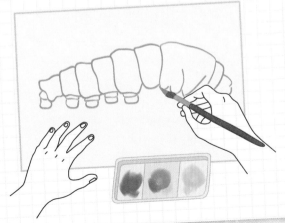

Feeding machines

Have you ever watched a caterpillar munch away nonstop on a leaf? If so, you may not be surprised to learn that it can increase its body weight at least one hundred times in just a few weeks. The tiny caterpillar begins eating as soon as it hatches from an egg.

A caterpillar's jaws are built for slicing into leaves.

The meal begins

The caterpillar grasps the leaf between its legs and starts to eat. Caterpillars are always hungry. The more the caterpillar eats, the more it grows.

The caterpillar stretches out its head and chews down toward its body.

The caterpillar disguises itself as a leaf to fool its enemies.

Halfway there

Having finished one leaf, the caterpillar moves on to another. It eats the softer, juicier parts first.

MAKE YOUR OWN CATERPILLAR RESTAURANT

You can study caterpillars eating in their natural habitat by keeping them in a fine mesh tube along with a low branch of their foodplant. You will need a piece of muslin or net, needle and thread, string, and scissors for this.

Ask an adult for help when using scissors.

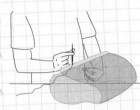

1. Sew the longest edges of a rectangular piece of muslin together to make a tube.

2. Find a branch that has feeding caterpillars on it and carefully slip the muslin tube over it. Tie the tube at both ends.

3. Check how much the caterpillars eat and grow each day. Move them to a new branch of the right foodplant when they finish these leaves.

All finished

The caterpillar has now nearly finished the third leaf. It will move on to another shoot if there are not enough leaves left on this one.

Nothing is safe

Caterpillars don't find their food only in the garden. Some moth caterpillars eat wood, some dine on cotton, and others eat house dust. Some even nibble feathers!

Changing skin

Butterflies and moths go through four stages in their lives. The third stage is the pupa, which is also called the chrysalis (*kris-a-lis*). This is when a caterpillar changes into an adult. As a caterpillar grows it sheds its skin four or five times. When it has eaten enough, it outgrows its skin for the last time and turns into a pupa. An adult butterfly or moth will emerge from this pupa.

Like a leaf

This may look like an old, wrinkled leaf, but it is really a comma butterfly's pupa suspended from a twig. It has shiny silver spots that sparkle in the light and make the pupa look empty inside.

The pupa stays very still, but lots of changes are taking place inside the case.

Many moth caterpillars spin a silken case, called a cocoon, to protect the pupa. Most predators cannot break through the strong silk.

Finding pupae

You might see pupae on leaves, twigs, bark, and even underground. Caterpillars climb down trees, wriggle through the soil, and hollow out a little space for themselves, where they change into a pupa.

Splitting its skin

After the caterpillar of the swallowtail butterfly finds a place to pupate, or turn into a pupa, it holds on with its hind legs and spins a silken thread. This strong thread supports the caterpillar while it waits a few hours for its final skin to split.

The silken thread, called a girdle, wraps around the caterpillar's body.

The caterpillar shrinks and tightens up as the pupa begins to form under its skin.

Once the pupa skin hits the air, it starts to harden.

New skin, old skin

The caterpillar has to wriggle around to slip out of its old skin. As the new pupa skin forms, the caterpillar skin falls down to the bottom.

Back legs grip the twig.

Can you see the wings? They are developing inside the pupa.

Empty caterpillar skin

Final form

The pupa of the swallowtail butterfly can be either green or brown to match its surroundings. This one looks like a green leaf attached to a twig. Turn to the next page to see a butterfly hatch from its pupa.

The perfect insect

The final stage in the metamorphosis of a butterfly or moth is very exciting. The insect that emerges from the pupa is very different from the caterpillar that made it. A total transformation has taken place. Keep a lookout for pupae ready to hatch. You will not be disappointed with what follows.

Hatching time

Look for a pupa with a split in it. This is a sure sign that things are about to happen! First the legs and antennae will appear from this split, followed shortly after by the rest of the body.

Split in pupa

Wing patterns are sometimes visible through a pupa that is ready to hatch.

Antenna

Crumpled and soft

Once it has emerged, the wet and delicate insect crawls to a place on the empty pupa from where it can hang downward to dry out.

Wings are crumpled and wet.

Pump, pump

The butterfly pumps blood from its body to the veins in its soft wings. This allows the wings to expand to their full size.

Once the wings have reached full size, the butterfly opens and closes them until they are completely dry.

Red rain

As the butterfly dries out, waste fluid is squirted from its body. In some species, such as the painted lady, this fluid is red. If a group of butterflies emerge from their pupae at the same time, it looks as though it is raining blood onto the ground below!

Ready for takeoff

The wings reach full size in about 30 minutes, but they still have to harden. About an hour later, the butterfly is ready to take to the air in search of food. Butterflies do not eat leaves. They drink nectar from their favorite flowers instead.

Silk cocoons

Moths, like butterflies, spend the third stage of their life cycle as a pupa. Many moth caterpillars spin a cocoon to protect them while they pupate. Silkworms—which are not really worms at all, but the caterpillars of the silkmoth—spin a very fine silken thread to make their cocoons with. We use this thread to weave delicate clothes.

The silkworm begins to spin a silken thread that comes out through holes under its head.

As the silkworm continues to spin silk, the cocoon gets thicker.

Cosy corner
The silkworm chooses a safe, cosy place to spin its cocoon. This can take two days, and the silken thread can be 2,600 ft (800 m) long by the time the cocoon is finished.

The cocoon is now strong enough to protect the silkworm as it changes into a pupa.

Fussy eaters
Silkworms are very fussy about their food. Only mulberry leaves will do. Silkworms would starve rather than eat anything else!

Soft but tough
The pure silk thread produced by silkworms is sometimes used for making parachutes, as well as fine clothes.

You will not find silkmoths in the wild. They are bred only for their silk on special farms.

Breaking out
Soon after the silkworm has changed into a pupa, it is ready to hatch. To do this, the moth makes a hole at one end of the cocoon by dissolving the threads with a special fluid. As soon as it has crawled out, the moth starts to expand and dry its wings.

Sensitive feathery antennae help the male detect a special scent given off by the female moth.

Hole where the moth crawled out

Leave me alone!

Butterflies and moths are very good at letting their enemies know that they do not want to be eaten. Hungry birds, spiders, reptiles, and small mammals are often scared away by aggressive displays. And the bright colors and markings of many butterflies and moths warn predators that they will taste rather nasty.

I've got my eye on you!

This fierce-looking owl butterfly frightens its enemies by displaying a large "eye" on its wing. It makes it look more like an angry lizard than a delicate insect.

Resting on a leaf, this butterfly could be mistaken for a lizard's eye.

Dead smelly

When disturbed, the white ermine moth pretends to be dead. If this does not work, it produces drops of foul-smelling yellow liquid.

Spot the difference!

Some harmless butterflies mimic, or copy, poisonous ones. The pattern and vivid colors of the monarch butterfly warn birds that it is poisonous. The harmless viceroy butterfly mimics the monarch's markings to trick hungry birds. Not many will risk a bite to find out which is which!

White spots on the monarch's head and thorax are a signal to predators of the butterfly's awful taste.

The viceroy has a black line on its hind wing. What other differences can you see?

Caught in the act

Sometimes false eyes are not enough to protect butterflies and moths from predators. This butterfly was too busy drinking nectar to notice the spider creeping up on it.

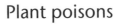
Spider

False eye

The caterpillar is unharmed by the poisons from its foodplant.

Plant poisons

The monarch caterpillar stores poisons from its foodplant—the deadly milkweed—in its body. These poisons are passed on to the butterfly during metamorphosis.

43

Hide and seek

Not all butterflies and moths are brightly colored to warn enemies that they are poisonous. In fact, most moths—and some butterflies—are quite dull in color. These insects have found another way of protecting themselves. Just like caterpillars, these adults use camouflage to hide from birds and reptiles. This lets them blend in with the shapes, patterns, and colors of trees, rocks, or leaves.

Bark blender

Birds would have a hard job finding this little moth from tropical rain forests. It is quite safe resting on the tree trunk—as long as it keeps still!

The patterns and colors of the moth's wings help it blend in with the tree trunk.

Genius of disguise

Perfect in shape and color, this Indian leaf butterfly blends in completely with the leaves it copies. Imagine how difficult it would be for a bird to find!

Veins on the butterfly's wings look just like veins on leaves.

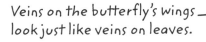

Light-colored marks on wing tips look like the broken end of a twig.

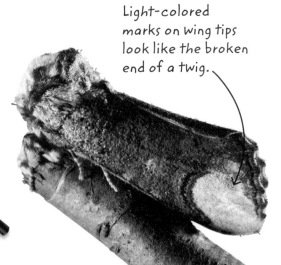

MOTH DETECTIVE

Finding camouflaged moths can be difficult. But with a little detective work, you may spot some. Search on tree trunks or fences for camouflaged moths. See how many you can find, but try not to disturb them.

Broken twig?

The shape and color of this buff tip moth make it look like a broken twig on a tree. As long as it stays still, it is safe from enemies searching for a meal.

Escaping the weather

On a cold day, you might feel like staying in bed or moving somewhere that is warm. Just like you, butterflies and moths try to avoid the cold. Some hibernate—this means finding a sheltered spot and spending the winter asleep. Others form huge groups and fly to warmer places to escape the cold. This movement is called migration.

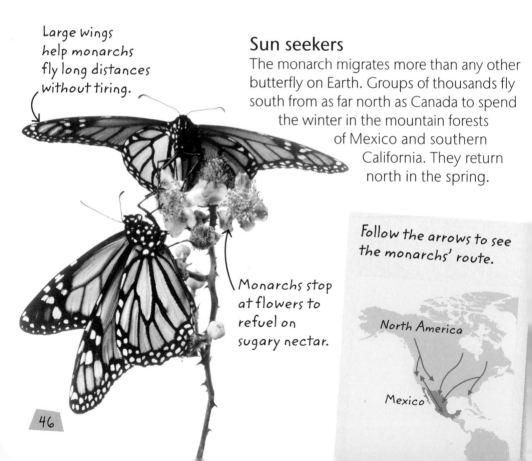

Large wings help monarchs fly long distances without tiring.

Sun seekers
The monarch migrates more than any other butterfly on Earth. Groups of thousands fly south from as far north as Canada to spend the winter in the mountain forests of Mexico and southern California. They return north in the spring.

Monarchs stop at flowers to refuel on sugary nectar.

Follow the arrows to see the monarchs' route.

North America

Mexico

Millions of monarchs

Migrating monarchs rest together on pine trees high up in the mountains. Sometimes they are covered with snow for many days. If you stayed outside for so long you would die, but a chemical in the butterflies' blood keeps them from freezing to death.

Masses of hanging butterflies cover the tree for several months.

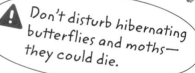

⚠ Don't disturb hibernating butterflies and moths— they could die.

Just hanging around

Peacocks and small tortoiseshells hang upside down when they hibernate. Look for them in garden sheds, hollow trees, and even inside houses. They do not eat or move for six months until the spring.

Flying fan

The painted lady is one of the toughest butterflies in the world—it can travel up to 620 miles (1,000 km).

In the garden

Filled with colorful, sweet-smelling flowers, gardens attract lots of butterflies by day and moths at night. In the summer, you'll see caterpillars attacking leaves, moths hiding in tree bark, and butterflies sunbathing on flowers. During the winter, a few of these insects seek shelter indoors—but they may come out for a visit on warm days.

Large skipper
If your garden has lots of colorful flowers, you might see some large skippers fluttering about. At rest, the fore and hind wings of these butterflies are held at different angles

Garden guest
The brimstone moth is a familiar garden visitor. It hides by day, but may come out to find a new resting spot. At dusk, look for the moth flying around the lights of houses.

This hawthorn leaf is a good place for the moth to lay its eggs.

ATTRACTING BUTTERFLIES

By choosing plants that caterpillars like to eat you can attract butterflies into your garden. Try planting some nettles in a sunny spot by a wall or corner. How many different butterflies can you spot?

⚠️ Wear gloves when planting nettles—they can sting.

Fast feeders

Elephant hawk-moth caterpillars eat plenty of leaves and flowers in their short lives. They do much of their feeding at night, but may eat garden plants such as fuchsias during the day. If disturbed, they swell up the front of their body like a big balloon.

Skeleton leaves

Peacock, red admiral, small tortoiseshell, and comma butterflies all lay their eggs on nettle leaves. The caterpillars eat so much, they make the nettles look like skeletons!

Red admiral resting in the sunshine

In the woodlands

Woodlands are one of the best places to look for butterflies and moths. You'll find butterflies fluttering on flowers in sunny glades or resting on twigs and branches, and moths hiding in leaf litter on the ground. Look for caterpillars feeding on leaves and plants—some hungry moth caterpillars cause a lot of damage by stripping the leaves from trees.

The silver-washed fritillary sunbathes with its orange-spotted wings open.

Top of the tree

On hot summer days, look for purple hairstreaks and silver-washed fritillaries near oak trees. They stay in the canopy, which is the top of the tree, when it is sunny. They also sunbathe on oak leaves near paths and clearings when it is warm.

The purple hairstreak's shiny wings change color in the sunshine.

Fun in the sun

Like most butterflies, the heath fritillary loves sunshine. It hardly moves in dull weather, but comes out to sunbathe in sunny woodland glades when it's hot. It lays its eggs on cow-wheat or plantain.

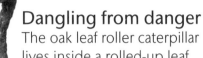

Dangling from danger

The oak leaf roller caterpillar lives inside a rolled-up leaf. When ants threaten, it throws itself off the leaf and dangles on a silk thread it has spun. When the coast is clear, the caterpillar crawls back up the thread onto the leaf, just like a mountaineer climbing up a rope.

Follow the leader

Pine processionary caterpillars set off in a line to look for food—the front caterpillar spins a thread of silk, which the others follow. After they have separated and eaten, the caterpillars fall into line again and follow the thread of silk back to the nest.

On the edge

The Danaid eggfly butterfly can be found in many different places, including Australia and North America. It only lives on sunny woodland edges and clearings—you'll find it visiting flowers such as lantanas and zinnias to sip nectar.

In the mountains

Walk through a mountain meadow in the summer, and you'll find it alive with butterflies and moths. However, mountain weather changes quickly. Dark clouds, snow flurries, and high winds can come in minutes, and insects in the mountains have to work hard to adapt to these sudden weather changes.

High and low
Most predators won't touch the poisonous monarch butterfly. You'll find it in the lowlands as well as on mountaintops.

Greasy wings
The small apollo butterfly has a special survival feature for life in the mountains. It has greasy wings, which means that it can survive freezing weather and sudden snow flurries.

Look for the small apollo on high mountains in Europe and Asia.

Black spots trap the Sun's heat.

Thick hairs keep the insect warm.

52

Mountain glory

The Bhutan (*boo-tan*) glory butterfly lives in the mountains of India and Thailand. The tails on the insect's wings are important. Predators see these first and peck them, leaving the more important parts of the insect alone.

Look for three long tails on the hind wing.

Warm and windy

Many mountain insects survive the cold winter by sunbathing during the day. But strong winds can turn a sunny day into a windy nightmare. This scarce copper butterfly clings to a rock to avoid being blown away.

Tough moth

Nothing is hardier than a burnet moth. Look for this red and black survivor in the mountains of Central America, Asia, and Europe. It tastes so bad that birds spit it out immediately, leaving large numbers of caterpillars and moths to survive and breed.

In the rain forest

No other place in the world has as many colourful butterflies and moths as the tropical rain forest. Lots of rainfall and a variety of plants make rain forests an ideal home for these insects. The best places to spot butterflies and moths are in sunny spots by riverbanks, in clearings, and around flowers.

Butterfly or moth?
It looks like a butterfly, and flies by day like a butterfly, but it's really a moth. This uranid moth lives in the Amazon rain forest in South America.

Butterfly-shaped wings glitter in the sunshine.

You can tell this is not a butterfly by the antennae—they have no clubs at the tips.

This nero butterfly sticks its proboscis into the damp sand to find water.

Water seekers
Male butterflies have to drink lots of water that is rich in salts. They need these salts to make special scents for attracting mates. Every few seconds they squirt out any excess water.

Invisible wings

Glasswing butterflies are very hard to spot—their see-through wings make them look invisible. This disguise works so well that some moths have copied it.

Delicate wing patterns help to camouflage this butterfly.

Two-headed caterpillar

In the rain forest, you may spot a caterpillar that looks like it has two heads. Its back end has a horn and a funny face to confuse birds and lizards—they never know which end to attack!

Flashy flier

Look for this flashy malachite (_mal-ah-kite_) butterfly flying around the open areas of a rain forest. It loves to visit flowers and drink their sweet nectar.

Safety in numbers

Lots of rain forest caterpillars live in groups. The bigger the group, the safer they are. As well as living in groups, these cup moth caterpillars are covered with poisonous spines, so predators keep their distance.

In the desert

You may not see many butterflies or moths flying around the desert in the middle of the day. Most of them seek shelter to avoid the heat of the midday sun. The best time to watch for butterflies and moths is in the morning or the evening. Look for them flying around water holes where grasses and wildflowers grow.

A long wait
A butterfly waits for the rain to fall before emerging from its pupa. In the hot, dry desert, this can take several years.

A smelly drink
For butterflies and moths to survive on the dry plains of Africa, they have to find water every day. This African ringlet even drinks from animal droppings!

The gray-brown color makes this butterfly invisible in the sandy, rocky desert.

Look for caterpillars feeding on the leaves of yucca plants.

Yucca feeders

After hatching, caterpillars of the yucca skipper butterfly tie the leaves of the yucca plant together with silk. They feed inside the leaves, safely hidden from predators. Later, they eat inside the plant and bore into its roots.

Escaping the heat

Flying in the early morning sun, and again in the cool of the evening, this little tiger blue butterfly escapes the scorching desert sun. At midday, it rests under a rock and keeps very still, so it does not get exhausted from the heat.

The shiny spots on the front wings reflect the sunlight and keep enemies away.

Phantom of the desert

As the Sun sets in the Australian desert, look for the large ghost moth flying around in search of food and water. Its light colors and long wings make it look just like a scary phantom.

In the Arctic

It would be very difficult for us to withstand the freezing winters, strong winds, and short summers of the Arctic. However, a few butterflies and moths live there all year round. They have special survival features such as antifreeze in their blood, and dark colors to absorb heat quickly.

Summer flier

This Arctic clouded yellow butterfly flies when the Sun is shining. As soon as the clouds come out, it seeks shelter. A special liquid in its blood keeps it from freezing, like the antifreeze in a car's radiator.

When temperatures fall below freezing, Arctic pupae remain safe inside protective silk cocoons.

The long hairs on its body help to keep the butterfly warm.

Summer feast

You'll find lots of butterflies visiting flowers during the short Arctic summer. Butterflies depend on flowers for sugary nectar. But they must be careful— many hungry birds and spiders are waiting nearby.

Catching rays

To make the most out of the weak Arctic sunshine, the Arctic woodland ringlet stretches out its wings across a rock and warms itself. Dark colors and heat already trapped in the rock also keep the butterfly warm.

At rest on a rock

Most Arctic moths spend their nights making low, short flights from flower to flower. They have to hide by day to avoid being eaten. This moth stays perfectly still on a rock, relying on its camouflage to pass undetected.

Index

Acknowledgments

DK Publishing would like to thank:

Sharon Grant and Wilfrid Wood for design assistance. Michele Lynch for editorial assistance and research. Linda Martin for editorial work on initial stages of book. Jane Parker and Helen Peters for the index.

Monarch
butterfly